Empowered

Empowered

DISCOVERING THE POWER
OF THE HOLY SPIRIT

Robert W. Clanton

Unless otherwise noted, all biblical quotations are taken from the New King James Bible, © 1982, 1983, 1985, 1994 by Thomas Nelson, Inc.

Copyright © 2015 Robert W. Clanton
All rights reserved
ISBN-10: 1514127202
ISBN-13: 9781514127209

I Love you Always DAD!! :)

Dedication

To my wife
Martha
Her joy has been my daily inspiration in carrying forward the great goals and aspirations God gave us so many years ago. Her unflagging belief in the power of prayer and the ministry of the Holy Spirit have served to underscore the importance of that which I herein contribute.

Contents

Acknowledgments ·ix
Introduction ·xi
Chapter 1 You Shall Receive Power· · · · · · · · · · · · · · · · · · 1
Chapter 2 The Promise is to You · · · · · · · · · · · · · · · · · · 5
Chapter 3 What is the Baptism in the Holy Spirit? · · · · · · · · 11
Chapter 4 Releasing the Gifts of the Spirit· · · · · · · · · · · · · 23
Chapter 5 Walking in the Spirit · · · · · · · · · · · · · · · · · · · 33
Conclusion: the Comforter has Come · · · · · · · · · · 37
Bibliography · 41

Acknowledgments

There are so many individuals who come to my mind who have helped in the production of this work. I want to thank Tom Johnson and Dr. Steve Crowther whose work in Grace College of Divinity has encouraged me to put words on paper and move toward publication. There are those who have served as examples of Spirit-filled, Spirit-led living: Michael Fletcher, Clem Ferris, and Ben Goodman as well as a host of friends. My fellow-elders at New Life Community Church have assisted and supported every step. Most importantly, my wife Martha has read and reread the manuscript always making helpful recommendations and correcting my numerous errors.

Introduction

THE WORLD AT ITS WORST needs the church at its best. We live in dramatically desperate days. Isaiah prophesied that *"when the enemy comes in like a flood, the Spirit of the Lord will raise up a standard against him"* (Isaiah 59:19). Daily news tells us of cultural and moral decay of historic dimensions. Meanwhile the church of Jesus Christ is challenged to function with New Testament vitality. In many places the question for the church is not success but survival. It is time for a re-birth of New Testament Christianity.

The great need of the church today is not for better methods and programs. Our greatest need is spiritual power. This is not a structural thing; it is a personal thing. A Spirit-empowered church is made up of Spirit-empowered individuals. The church must once again become the house in which the Holy Spirit is active and working.

My aim in this short book is not corporate church renewal, although I certainly hope such will come. My aim is individuals. Corporate re-vitalization can only happen when the people who inhabit the church find new empowerment. The flame starts in human hearts.

I invite you to explore the Spirit-filled life. This is not a magical, mystical tour. It is not a walk on the wild side. It is a solid, biblical relationship with Jesus Christ that will empower and enable you to live with greater joy and freedom. So, let the adventure begin.

CHAPTER 1

You Shall Receive Power

WHAT DOES IT MEAN TO be filled with the Holy Spirit? How can I receive all that God has for me? These are important questions every Christian should ask.

After all, Jesus Himself spoke often about the Holy Spirit – about how His followers should become intimately acquainted with the Comforter. He described *"rivers of living water"* (John 7:38) that would flow from our hearts. When it came time for Him to depart this earth, He gave instructions for the disciples to wait in Jerusalem until they were *"endued with power from on high."* (Luke 24:49, Acts 1:4) His words found fulfillment on the Day of Pentecost. The Holy Spirit was poured out. It is now for us today to discover the wonderful provision of the Promise of the Father – the Spirit-filled, Spirit-empowered life.

THE THIRSTY MAY COME

I find today a host of people interested and thirsty for more of the Holy Spirit. At the same time, there are entire churches where mention of the Holy Spirit causes knee-jerk reactions of fear and cynicism. On one hand, many folks are being drawn toward a fuller relationship with the third Person of the Trinity. On the other hand, many are afraid, thinking it will change everything and destroy all the good things they now know.

But, Jesus calls us! He beckons us to the real thing. He tells us He has paved the way to a Spirit-filled life. We cannot ignore it. We need not fear it. We must be ready for what God wants to do. Like the water level rising in a river, the presence of God is increasing in His Church. We need to go deeper and learn more how to walk in the Holy Spirit. Whether Baptist or Methodist, Catholic or even Pentecostal, God is calling us to a fuller relationship with Himself. It will not destroy our heritage. It will only enrich it.

The Fulfillment

Jesus' words to the disciples about power were fulfilled on the Day of Pentecost when God's Spirit came down. It was dramatic and earth-shaking.

> *[2] And suddenly there came a sound from heaven, as of a rushing mighty wind, and it filled the whole house where they were sitting. [3] Then there appeared to them divided tongues, as of fire, and one sat upon each of them. [4] And they were all filled with the Holy Spirit and began to speak with other tongues, as the Spirit gave them utterance.* Acts 2:2-4

The decisive moment of release in terms of power and ministry was this baptism in the Holy Spirit that came on the Day of Pentecost. The Great Commission (Matt. 28:18-20), the Cross, and the entire life of Jesus all pointed toward this coming of the Comforter. The enduement with power around 9am that morning was not only the promise of the Father, but the fullness and application of all Jesus came to do in us and through us. We need this.

From that moment forward, the disciples were catapulted into a new realm. Weak, hesitant Peter was transformed into the man of God who stood before thousands to testify. Former cowardly disciples were morphed into martyrs who would turn their world upside down. Angry zealots became apostles of peace. Timid souls became world-changers. From that small upper room they then carried the Word about Jesus to the cultures of that day. It is important to note that they could *not* have done this without the needed power – the Holy Spirit.

We are the same way. As Christians, you and I were designed to run by Spirit-power. Without Him, we are powerless. We may look good and sound good, but we are unable to live His way. It's like a car without gasoline. It may be sleek and shiny, but it doesn't run. We were made to be Spirit-filled and Spirit-empowered.

He is at Work Today

I believe that the Holy Spirit is working in every Bible-believing, Christ exalting church. Unfortunately, in many cases, He must work as something of a covert agent. His role is limited to a certain predetermined scope of theological and cultural acceptability. "We don't believe that here." "We don't practice that here." Amazingly, the Holy Spirit does not totally withdraw when He is limited, quenched, or redirected. He simply works in secret.

As an example, I know hundreds of instances in which the gifts of the Spirit are operational in churches that theologically say they do not believe in the present-day operation of such supernatural gifts. There are countless examples of vibrant Spirit-filled activities ranging from healing to tongues to prophecy that take place in church environments where they are structurally suppressed. I have heard preachers and teachers deliver clear, anointed prophetic words while at the same time declaring that they do not believe prophecy takes place today!

It is time to welcome the Holy Spirit in His fullness. He will not harm us. He will do exactly what Jesus said He will do. He will illuminate us. He will empower us. He will take the words and work of Jesus and declare it, disclose it, and deliver it to us (John 16:14).

I am not here addressing the operation of the Holy Spirit in the church service on Sunday morning, but rather in the heart of the believer. I understand the need for certain things allowed or not allowed IN the church service. Paul believed that, too. He teaches in depth about this in I Corinthians 14:6-33. Each church must decide for itself how the Holy Spirit will work in the corporate gathering (example: altar calls, praying for the sick, open microphone or closed, levels of exuberance, who determines the flow of the service, etc.). When I call us to welcome the Holy Spirit, I am not condoning free-wheeling unscriptural activities in the church service. I think far too many people and churches equate Holy Spirit activity with weirdness (swing from the chandeliers, holy rolling, and such). The Holy Spirit is a gentleman and always operates in a certain kind of order. It is the flesh that can really get weird – not the Spirit.

So, don't think about church right now. Think about you! Don't worry about something strange in a church service making you uncomfortable. Let's go to the private place of your own heart and ask for more of the Holy Spirit. He will meet you there. It's time to dive in asking the Holy Spirit to fill you to the full. "Come Holy Spirit! Have Your way!"

Discussion Questions:

1. In what ways is the ministry of the Holy Spirit like a river?
2. Why do you think people are afraid of the Holy Spirit?
3. Can you tell ways the Holy Spirit has transformed your life?
4. Can you describe a time when the Holy Spirit was working powerfully in your church service?

CHAPTER 2

The Promise is to You

A ONE-TIME EVENT?
WAS THE DAY OF PENTECOST a one-time event never to be repeated? Or, is it the pattern for power carrying forward through Church History – to be experienced afresh by every church and every individual throughout the church age?

I believe it is both. Yes, the Day of Pentecost was a one-time event. For the first time, the Holy Spirit was poured out upon all flesh (Joel 2:28), not just a few Old Testament prophets here and there – an occasional interruption that happened to especially holy individuals. The Holy Spirit was poured out without measure on all of God's people. In that sense, the Church was once for all baptized in the Holy Spirit. A new era was inaugurated. It was momentous.

The exact particulars of Pentecost may not ever find exact reproduction. We need not see again and again an actual ball of fire. We do not require the speaking of known foreign languages. We may not hear the fury of a *"rushing mighty wind"* (Acts 2:4). There is definitely a uniqueness about the first Pentecost.

But, in another sense, that baptism must be made current for every one of us. Its particulars may not be repeated, but its essence MUST. If anything in Church History is clear, the tendency to lose power is evident. We must experience a fresh empowering of the Holy Spirit with every generation, with every year, with every moment. As Dr. James D.G. Dunn says in his classic work, *Baptism in the Holy Spirit*:

> In a sense, therefore, Pentecost can never be repeated – for the new age is here and cannot be ushered in again. But in another sense Pentecost, or rather the experience of Pentecost, can and must be repeated in the experience of all who would become Christians.[1]

We must *experience* this once for all baptism in the Holy Spirit. We must make it ours.

John Stott states this another way. In terms of what happened at Pentecost, he says two things are evident: the story is DESCRIPTIVE and PRESCRIPTIVE, formative and normative. Acts 2 describes the unique first coming of the Holy Spirit upon the Church. But, how much of the Day of Pentecost is a prescription for the coming church age – for us? Dr. Stott reminds us of Peter's own words in Acts 2:39.

> *For the promise is to you and to your children, and to all who are afar off, as many as the Lord our God will call.* Acts 2:39 (NKJV)

He goes on to add, "In this sense those converted on the Day of Pentecost … were typical of all subsequent believers."[2] The Day of Pentecost, while certainly unusual in many ways, is a pattern for power to the Church today.

---

[1] Dunn, James D.G. *Baptism in the Holy Spirit* (Philadelphia: Westminster Press, 1970) p. 53.
[2] Stott, John R.W. *Baptism & Fullness: the Work of the Holy Spirit Today* (Downers Grove, IL: Intervarsity Press, 1964) p. 30. John Stott writes from the perspective that "the baptism in the Holy Spirit" takes place at conversion along with the forgiveness of sins. He differentiates between the reception of the Spirit and the various manifestations of the Spirit. He calls the reception of the Holy Spirit at Pentecost a mandatory PRESCRIPTION, while the gifts listed in Acts are mere DESCRIPTIONS of what happened then.

Terminology

At issue is this term BAPTISM IN THE HOLY SPIRIT. But, in a larger sense, the issue is not the term, but the power, the vibrancy, the presence of the Spirit of God in the Church.

Each church and each denomination may define Holy Spirit baptism differently. But, there remains an important invitation to all followers of Jesus: BE FILLED WITH THE SPIRIT.

When this topic comes up, the devil loves to cloud the air. I grew up in a denomination that did not talk much about the Holy Spirit. We were big on Bible and salvation in Jesus, but the Holy Spirit was a vague topic. By contrast, there were other denominations that seemed to talk ONLY about the Holy Spirit. In fact, some used strange terminology like, "get the Holy Ghost" (using old King James terminology). It seemed to me: one group ignored, minimized, or under-emphasized the Spirit, while the other group magnified and over-emphasized Him. It's time for a biblical, blessed, and balanced understanding of the Spirit-empowered life!

Who is He?

The Holy Spirit is the third Person of the Trinity. Father, Son, and Holy Spirit comprise the Godhead and are three-in-one. If we look at the history of divine revelation, the Bible falls into three sections:

1) Old Testament
2) Gospels
3) Acts and the rest of the New Testament.

The Father is the predominant Person of the Old Testament. **The Son** is the focus of the Gospels. Then from Acts on through the end of the New Testament, the primary Person at work is **the Holy Spirit**. We today live in the era of the Holy Spirit.

That is not to say that the Father and the Son are not at work. Of course, they are! But as we read the Scripture, we find in the economy of God, the Holy Spirit is center stage in the Gospel ministry of empowering the Church and reaching the world. In fact, the Book of Acts, while named the Acts of the Apostles, has also been called the Acts of the Holy Spirit – and there is no "Amen" at the end of Acts. It continues today.

This is That.
At the outset of the Apostolic Age, Simon Peter stood up and declared,

> *This is that which was spoken by the prophet Joel, "And it shall come to pass in the last days, says the Lord, that I will pour out of My Spirit on all flesh." (Acts 2:28)*

In so doing, Peter did two things: 1) he identified the last days, and 2) he described the primary biblical characteristic of those days.

Much has been written and said about "the last days." People want to know the signs of the times and how near the end might be. According to Peter, the last days began over 2,000 years ago! That does not mean the events of current history do not hint about the nearness of the Second Coming. It does however mean that the focus of any end-time people should be on the power of the Spirit rather than the pulse of politics and world events.

On the Day of Pentecost, God sounded the starting gun for the Church in "end-times ministry." To accomplish this, He provided "end-times power." The race will continue until the Second Coming. We are empowered by the Holy Spirit to stand against darkness and live in light – to rise above death and walk in life – to carry the Gospel to the ends of the earth. We are enabled to live out the Gospel and to shine the light into a world destined for judgment.

In order to fulfill her mandate, the Church needs the Holy Spirit. He is our mode of operation. The primary characteristic of the New Testament church should be the power and presence of the Holy Spirit. That is not to say that we preach the Spirit. No! We preach Jesus! But we preach Him by the power of the Holy Spirit. This is not a fleshly, human undertaking. It is a Spirit-empowered calling.

Discussion Questions:

1. How is the Holy Spirit like fire?
2. How is the Holy Spirit like wind?
3. For you, what is the most interesting aspect of the Day of Pentecost as described in Acts Chapter 2?
4. Why do you think there is so much confusion over the ministry of the Holy Spirit?

CHAPTER 3

What is the Baptism in the Holy Spirit?

The Baptism in the Holy Spirit

When, at the Jordan River, John the Baptist first identified Jesus, he made an important prediction. Luke 3 tells us that while John baptized in water, Jesus would baptize in the Holy Spirit. John said,

> *I indeed baptize you with water; but One mightier than I is coming, whose sandal strap I am not worthy to loose. He will baptize you with the Holy Spirit and fire.* Luke 3:16

In John's words, the ultimate expectation of Jesus' ministry would be baptizing followers in the Holy Spirit.

Our evangelical sensibilities may be shocked here. Surely, John had it wrong. Jesus came to die on the Cross and rise from the dead saving us from our sins. The defining characteristic and end of Jesus' ministry must be the Cross! This view holds that the Holy Spirit and the Cross are two separate events. Jesus came to save us from our sins, and only later for a few super-saints there might be a "second work of grace" to fill them (baptize them) with the Holy Spirit. The Cross and the Upper Room are two separate realities – two separate experiences. Often times, people might say "I got saved and then years later I got baptized in the Holy Spirit."

In fact, when you hear my own story, you might say this is exactly what happened to me. I was born again at an early age – 7 years old lying on my bed one night. But it was not until I was 19, on a baseball field that I was catapulted into the Spirit-filled, Spirit-empowered life.

Terminology notwithstanding, the essence of this view is a separation between two major events in the life of the believer. John the Baptist did not break up our relationship with Jesus into two separate stages. He shoots for everything in one massive move! Included are Cross, the Resurrection, AND the Upper Room! While far too many of us drag this process out over years, God's desire is for us to come full-force into the Kingdom of God in a three-fold foundation of conversion, water baptism, and infilling with the Holy Spirit.

From a broader perspective, everything about Jesus' teaching and ministry pointed toward the releasing of his disciples in apostolic ministry. He kept speaking about the Comforter that was yet to come. While the Cross was His own personal mission, He saw it as also pointing toward Pentecost when the disciples would be empowered, enlightened, renewed, and released. Jesus never divorced the Cross from the Upper Room. In the words of Dr. Dunn:

> The climax and purposed end of Jesus' ministry is not the cross and the resurrection, but the ascension and Pentecost… Pentecost was the climax of Jesus' ministry for the disciples.[3]

Jesus is not satisfied with us simply having a ticket to heaven. He wants us to be empowered by the Holy Spirit.

When Does It Happen?

How are we to interpret this? Different denominations describe Spirit-baptism in a variety of ways. Here is a quick survey of various views:

---
3   Dunn. P. 44.

What is the Baptism in the Holy Spirit?

1. The "Not for Today" group. These folks have problems with the term "baptism in the Holy Spirit,", and say that's in the past, never to be seen again. They might accept "infilling with the Holy Spirit" but theologically don't think Acts 2 is a reality for today.
2. The "Born Again" group. They are similar to the "Not for Today" folks, but accept "baptism in the Holy Spirit" as another term for getting saved. It happens when you are born again and does not include any supernatural gifts. In fact, they say, spiritual gifts are passed away, so don't expect them. At new birth, you get all there is – there is no more available or possible.
3. The "Confirmation" group. Others call it Confirmation. It is ritual in nature. Gifts and empowerment are subjugated to ritual. Liturgy, formality, and theology accommodate the idea of the presence of the Holy Spirit without any corresponding experience in the person.
4. The "Second Blessing" group. Still others call it a second work of grace after salvation that releases the believer into the supernatural realm by receiving the Holy Spirit. By this view, a person RECEIVES JESUS at salvation, and then RECEIVES THE HOLY SPIRIT at the baptism in the Holy Spirit. Only problem here is the fact that no one can even get saved without the work of the Holy Spirit in their heart. By this view, a person can be saved but not yet have the Holy Spirit. Romans 8:9[4] clearly says that there is no such thing as a Christian who does not have the Holy Spirit working in his heart.
5. The "Speak in Tongues" group. One final group goes into overdrive. They believe speaking in tongues is the singular evidence of Spirit-baptism and no one is even saved until they

---

[4] *"But you are not in the flesh but in the Spirit, if indeed the Spirit of God dwells in you. Now if anyone does not have the Spirit of Christ, he is not his."* Rom. 8:9 (NKJV)

"get the Holy Ghost." And, the singular sign of the Spirit's presence is the gift of tongues.

It's a mess. And there is mass confusion.

Terminology can hang us up and rob us of the powerful underlying truths of what God wants for us. So, let's cut through the fog and try to lay hold of the Spirit-filled, Spirit-empowered life. Whether we call it the baptism in the Holy Spirit or the fullness of the Spirit or the empowering of the Holy Spirit, the issue is not the name but rather the power.

I am inclined to believe in "progressive take-over." It includes powerful encounters with God but also may involve slow-opening friendship with the Holy Spirit. Each person might experience Him in their own individual way, but the end is the same – saturation with the Comforter. Baptism in the Holy Spirit is not so much a description of a one-time event as it is a vision of a Spirit-saturated life.

The Meaning of Baptism

When John the Baptist described the baptism in the Holy Spirit, he did not have a systematic theology book in his hand. He was not speaking of a singular doctrinal experience as if one might check it off and move on. He was describing the totality of Jesus' work in the believer. "Baptism in the Holy Spirit" included the full the scope of Jesus' ministry.

The classic picture of Spirit-baptism is a crisis event in which the recipient has a momentary breakthrough in which hands are laid on him/her, they feel a surge of power, and begin to utter words in an unknown tongue. Thus they are said to have received "the baptism in the Holy Spirit." This certainly has precedent both in Scripture and practical experience. But, is this the formula defining the entire scope of Spirit baptism? Is this the formula, or is it one expression of a bigger picture?

The word "baptize" means to immerse, to saturate, to dip, or to inundate.[5] Jesus came to do all this with respect to the Holy Spirit in our lives. This is no singular event of temporary emotionalism. This is not a one-time crisis experience followed by years of mediocrity. This is not an event to look back upon, but an experience to continue in.

Spirit, Soul, and Body

I Thessalonians 5:23 tells us that we are made of three parts: spirit, soul, and body. There we read,

> *Now may the God of peace Himself sanctify you completely; and may He preserve your whole spirit, soul, and body be preserved blameless at the coming of the Lord Jesus Christ.*

When we speak of salvation, this begins in your spirit. The Holy Spirit comes to inhabit your human spirit. You are born again. All believers in Jesus receive the Holy Spirit at salvation. This is your first personal encounter with the Third Person of the Trinity.

But what about the mind, emotions, and will (the components of what the Bible calls your "soul")?[6] These components of the soul are then the object of progressive sanctification that re-makes them in the image of Jesus. The power of God has arrived in the spirit of man, but there is always resistance to the things of God residing in the soul (mind, emotions, and will). The flesh wars against the spirit. Our carnality throws up continual roadblocks to spiritual

---

[5] Vine, W.E. *Vine's Expository Dictionary of New Testament Words* (McLean, VA: McDonald Publishing Co.) pgs. 98-100.
[6] Bennett, Dennis and Rita. *Trinity of Man* (Plainfield, NJ: Logos International, 1979) pgs. 44-45. A more in-depth treatment of the components of the soul may be found in the three volume work by Watchman Nee entitled *The Spiritual Man* (New York: Christian Fellowship Publishers, 1968).

growth and progress. A breakthrough is required to overcome the resistance that compresses and inhibits spiritual power.

When the Bible speaks of the Baptism in the Holy Spirit, I believe the scope is complete inundation and saturation of the human being in spiritual reality and power. This is our destiny. This is our mandate and calling. Our flesh wars against this. Our carnality robs us. Only the release of God's Spirit in every area of life can suffice and satisfy.

When we speak of the Baptism in the Holy Spirit we are not referring to something that is simply a one-time accomplishment. Rather, it is a calling to full surrender and saturation. For many this will involve the laying on of hands and prayer of faith that helps break the barriers of carnal resistance and allows the river of God's Spirit to freely flow out of the heart. For others, the release may come very quietly and seemingly naturally as the heart is yielded to God.

Receiving the Power

How does this baptism take place? We can find patterns in Scripture. We find examples with which we can identify.[7] Here are the basic steps:

1. Desire – hungry for God.

Jesus tells us in Matthew 5:6, *"Blessed are those who hunger and thirst for righteousness for they shall be filled."* Mary, in her beautiful song called The Magnificat, tells how God scatters the proud and puts down the mighty, but *"He has filled the hungry with good things."* (Luke 1:53) Again, Jesus practically shouts it to us:

---

[7] It is a fascinating and illuminating study to hear various individuals' stories of how the Holy Spirit has worked in their lives. I plan to release a future work in which such stories can be told.

> [37] *On the last and greatest day of the festival, Jesus stood and said in a loud voice,* **"Let anyone who is thirsty come to me and drink.** [38] *Whoever believes in me, as Scripture has said, rivers of living water will flow from within them." * [39] *By this he meant the Spirit, whom those who believed in him were later to receive. Up to that time the Spirit had not been given, since Jesus had not yet been glorified.* John 7:37-39 (NIV)

Of fundamental importance is that we be hungry and thirsty for more of God.

2. Prayer – ask God to fill you.

There are those who take the attitude, "If God wants me to have this, He can give it to me when He is ready." I have never seen God bless such an attitude. He demands that we sincerely ASK Him. Prayer is always an essential part of our relationship with God. Jesus said it this way:

> [9] *"So I say to you: Ask and it will be given to you; seek and you will find; knock and the door will be opened to you.* [10] *For everyone who asks receives; the one who seeks finds; and to the one who knocks, the door will be opened.* [11] *"Which of you fathers, if your son asks for a fish, will give him a snake instead?* [12] *Or if he asks for an egg, will give him a scorpion?* [13] *If you then, though you are evil, know how to give good gifts to your children, how much more will your Father in heaven* **give the Holy Spirit to those who ask him!***"* Luke 11:9-13 (NIV)

So, I will suggest a simple prayer you might pray. If the following prayer helps you formulate your thoughts and express them to God, then please use it. But, be sure that your prayer comes out of your own heart as you ask God to fill you with the Holy Spirit.

Lord, thank you that my sins are forgiven by the Blood of Jesus. Thank you that I have been accepted into Your family. I once again, repent of all my sins and I give myself completely to You.

I ask You now to fill me with the Holy Spirit. I claim Your promise that You will cause rivers of living water to flow from inside me. I yield myself completely to You.

I ask that You release all Your gifts in my life. I ask that You enable me to walk in Your power in a new way. I receive all that You have for me. It is in the Name of Jesus that I pray. Amen.

3. Believe – begin to thank God for His Gift and His gifts.

You must have faith in God and His answers. Too often people try to FEEL their way into God. Having repented and been forgiven – having prayed a scriptural prayer – they then wait for some sort of emotional jolt. They expect an immediate "lightning bolt" experience.

I acknowledge that some people do in fact have dramatic emotional surges at this point. But, not everyone does. Do not wait for some kind of pre-determined "buzz" to make you feel strange and different.

Instead, it is time to BELIEVE God's Word. Salvation is received by faith, and the infilling of the Holy Spirit is received by faith, too.

Jesus gave us this amazingly simple principle when He said, *"Therefore I tell you, whatever you ask for in prayer, believe that you have received it, and it will be yours."* Mark 11:24 (NIV). It sounds too good to be true, but that's the way God works. Faith is the currency of the Kingdom of God. Believing God and His Word releases all that He has to you. Without faith, the pipeline gets stopped up.

4. Hands laid on

Being filled with the Spirit can certainly happen when you are alone, but often God says you should get someone who is spiritually mature to lay hands on you for the receiving of God's power. This is a spiritual principle. In the Book of Acts, we find this often. Acts 8:17 says that when Peter and John ministered to the new converts in Samaria, they *"laid hands on them, and they received the Holy Spirit."* When a disciple named Ananias ministered to the newly converted Paul, Acts 9:17 says, *"...laying hands on him he (Ananias) said, 'Brother Paul...be filled with the Holy Spirit.'"* Then, when Paul was leading twelve disciples into a fuller relationship with God at Ephesus, Acts 19:6 says, *"...when Paul had laid hands on them, the Holy Spirit came upon them."*

There is something about being surrounded by strong believers that can bring release of the power of God. The laying on of hands is not a ritual. It is an act of faith whereby the faith of those around you joins with your faith to touch God.

5. Yield to the power of God

As God pours out His Spirit, there may be a sense in which you need to physically surrender to Him. By faith, begin to express gratitude for His priceless gift. Be willing to release a prayer language as God gives it to you. Some might tend to tense up at this moment. Instead, relax and rest in God, fully confident of His presence and power.

By faith, believe that God has answered your prayer. It is now time for you to accept His gifts with confidence. Doing so, you may begin to move with a new power and enablement that settles on you from God.

6. Communion and Community.

Your spiritual life is like an ember in a fire. If it stays around other red-hot coals, it will continue to burn. If however, it is separated from the fire, it quickly grows cold and dies. I find the same true for those who seek to be filled with the Holy Spirit.

After praying to receive the infilling of the Holy Spirit, you need to surround yourself with a spiritual atmosphere. You need to stay in the fire. I find this to be so important.

Many times, individuals pray for a deeper walk with God and come away feeling that they didn't get what they thought would come. They listen to dramatic stories from others and wonder why their experience didn't match up. Please remember, every person's experience is unique to them. No two stories are identical.

But this I know, if you stay in a Spirit-filled atmosphere, your faith will grow. If you stay in an environment in which spiritual life is rich, you will find your hidden inhibitions increasingly drop. Our preconceived notions of spiritual life can often be a blockage to receiving the real thing. That's why staying in a full worship experience where the Word of God is preached and believed – where believing prayer is practiced – where encouragement flows – will cause you to continue experiencing new levels of release.

7. Walk in Breakthrough.

I firmly believe that God wants to lead us ever higher. When, in the Gospels, Jesus ministered to people, it seems no two people had the same thing happen. One was healed immediately; another was touched while walking down the road later that day. Still another received a miracle from Jesus before He even showed up.

I have known of individuals who were awakened in the night by a breakthrough taking place in their spiritual life. One man I know was touched while riding his horse one day. You have entered into a life-long adventure in experiencing God the Holy Spirit. You have been catapulted into a new realm. For some, this may be an emotional experience. For others, it may unfold more subtly and manifest itself over time.

I believe this is a pattern not only for initial infilling, but for all spiritual progress. For me, this found traction at age 19. After years of vacillation, I committed my life to Christ, and sought more of His power and presence.

But, it didn't stop there. I have experienced again and again a fresh presence of the Holy Spirit as I found new places of surrender. It can happen numerous times in the unfolding of God's plan and calling. It is not just a one-time event, but an on-going reality in the life of a believer who wants to grow in God.

I have known believers who upon reaching new stages of life, have sought God for new power and been inundated in fresh truth and fresh fire. We might ask, "Were they baptized again in the Holy Spirit?" I would answer no, "They are further being baptized (immersed, saturated) in the Holy Spirit." It began at their salvation when the Holy Spirit first entered their life. It has progressed through kneeling at the altar, through the laying on of hands, through quiet moments of prayer, through high times of worship. We experience new eras of empowerment, and new steps of obedience. It continues toward full saturation.

FILLED WITH THE HOLY SPIRIT

As I have said, terminology can be an obstacle. I know of individuals who will not countenance discussion of "the baptism in the Holy Spirit" yet regularly embrace being "filled with the Holy Spirit." Theological language can cause unnecessary roadblocks.

Virtually all Bible-believing churches agree that we are called and commanded to "be filled with the Holy Spirit" (Eph. 5:18). The next question that must be answered is, "What does that mean?" "What is the result?" and "How do we walk in it?"

Once again, we need to address the matter of biblical terminology. There are several ways the Bible describes the action of the Holy Spirit in the life of the believer. In Acts, we read that He *"fell on them"* (Acts 10:44, 11:15). Other places He *"came upon them"* (Acts 19:6) or He is *"poured out"* (Acts 2:17). Is there one term that is all-encompassing? No doubt the pre-dominant word is *"filled"* (Acts 2:4, 4:8, 4:31, 13:9, 13:52), but what does all this signify?

The meaning of "filled with the Holy Spirit" is the idea of "controlled and enabled." The spirit of man is united with the Spirit of God at new birth. Then begins the process of the Spirit of God enforcing the rule of Christ in every area of life.

There are two dimensions of the Spirit-filled life: 1) gifts and 2) fruit.

Discussion Questions:

1. What does it mean to be hungry for more of God?
2. What is meant by the phrase, "Faith is the currency of the Kingdom of God?"
3. What are you supposed to do if you pray a simple prayer but don't feel that anything has happened to you yet?
4. How do you feel about having someone pray for you publicly or privately?
5. Why is it important to be in a strong, spiritual environment in order for you to grow in Christ?
6. Can you see a pattern in your life of how God has led you to new levels as you have grown in Him?

CHAPTER 4
Releasing the Gifts of the Spirit

Gifts for Today

Perhaps the most exciting (and controversial) aspect of Spirit-filled living is the release of the gifts of the Holy Spirit. Huge discussions (arguments) have been going on for decades about the availability of the supernatural today. Have the supernatural gifts passed away at the end of the apostolic age, or do they continue today? The two schools of thought are:

1. CESSATIONIST. The name of this group comes from the word "CEASE" and they believe the supernatural gifts of the Spirit ceased with the end of the apostolic age with the death of the last apostle.
2. CONTINUATIONIST. This is a big word that simply means "CONTINUE." This is the belief that supernatural actions (miracles, healing, casting out demons, tongues, and so forth) have not ceased but continue up until today.

I am a continuationist. I believe from Scripture and practical experience that God still works supernaturally through Christians today.

The definitions and number of these gifts may vary from one teacher to another, but virtually no one says all gifts are passed away. Virtually all agree that gifts of leadership, encouragement, and serving still operate (even the cessationists!). It is gifts such as healing, prophecy, and tongues that cause the stir. It is the supernatural gifts that constitute the divide between the cessationists and the continuationists.

Supernatural Gifts or Sanctified Talents

Going further, even among the continuationists, two difference schools have developed.

3. The EVANGELICAL view of the gifts of the Spirit. This group says that different gifts belong to different believers and no one should expect to have all the gifts. In fact, you might learn that you have three or four particular gifts and don't need to worry about the others. This school of thought can be very similar to personality types. The supernatural element is accommodated, but gifting is at times equated with natural talents.
4. The CHARISMATIC view of the gifts of the Spirit. This second group says that all gifts of the Spirit are equally available to all believers, and they are purely supernatural in essence. One cannot prepare or predict, but rather only be available. Such gifts are "spot-action" and unrelated to natural, "carnal" talents.

So which one is right? I believe both have elements of truth. Are spiritual gifts purely supernatural or can we practice them and improve them? I believe that all true spiritual gifts come only by the power of the Holy Spirit, but God also supernaturally uses our natural abilities. In addition, the more we practice them, the more proficient we can become. The more we use our gifting, the more that gifting is enriched and made fruitful.

It is a matter of increased sensitivity and responsiveness to the promptings of the Holy Spirit.

SPIRITUAL LANGUAGE

The most interesting question with respect to Spirit-baptism has to do with spiritual language. The phenomenon of speaking in tongues bears our consideration for several reasons. We need to know what it is and why God has given this unusual gift.

Early in the Pentecostal movement, an equation was established whereby baptism in the Holy Spirit and the gift of tongues became synonymous. Throughout the decades of Pentecostal and charismatic history, speaking in tongues has usually been identified as the "initial evidence" of Spirit-baptism. That is to say that the singular outward evidence and validation of the presence of the Holy Spirit was the gift of tongues. While I value all God's gifts and in no way want to discount them, I believe this view of tongues goes too far. Tongues is not the evidence of the presence of the Holy Spirit.

I believe that all of the gifts of the Holy Spirit are available today. But, is tongues the singular evidence of God's power released on a seeking believer? Increasingly, pastors, churches, denominations, and theologians agree that it is not – even among Pentecostal leaders. What then, is the place of tongues in the life of the Spirit-filled believer? This is so very important for us to understand.

In I Corinthians 12, Paul asks, *"Do all speak in tongues?"* Context dictates that the answer is "NO."

> [28] *And God has appointed these in the church: first apostles, second prophets, third teachers, after that miracles, then gifts of healings, helps, administrations, varieties of tongues.* [29] *Are all apostles?*

Are all prophets? Are all teachers? Are all workers of miracles? [30] *Do all have gifts of healings? Do all speak with tongues? Do all interpret?* I Corinthians 12:28-30

But, we need to put this in balance with other verses in this portion of Scripture. Later, in I Corinthians 14, Paul speaks of prophecy (another one of the gifts), and declares, *"You can all prophesy."* (I Corinthians 14:31) He repeatedly implies that the gift of prophecy is available to and functional through every believer present. (I Co. 14:23-24) What is Paul saying about the gift of prophecy? All CAN prophesy, but not everyone WILL prophesy. It is theoretically possible that every believe might and could prophesy, but realistically not everyone will.

He uses the same logic in respect to the gift of tongues. He acknowledges that not everyone will speak in tongues (I Co. 12:30). The nature of the gift of tongues will shed even more light on this. We will explore this a little later. While saying not everyone will speak in tongues, he then encourages *"I wish you all spoke with tongues..."* (I Co. 14:5) The pattern in the Book of Acts is that they "all" spoke with tongues (Acts 2:4; Acts 10:44-46; Acts 19:6). On the one hand, he says not everyone will speak with tongues, but on the other he says that he wants everyone to display this gift. Similar to prophecy, all CAN speak in tongues, but not every one WILL speak in tongues.

How are we to understand this? Pentecostal and charismatic denominations say tongues is NORMATIVE (i.e. you should speak in tongues), while others say it is COINCIDENTAL (i.e. you might – some do, some don't). Which is it?

There are two ways we need to approach the answer to this question. First, we must understand the nature of the gift of tongues. What is it? Then, we can identify the differences in practical use.

What is Tongues?

Scripture describes three different types or manifestations of the gift of tongues. The first is found in Acts 2 and is the most easily described. When the Spirit was poured out in the Upper Room, there were several dramatic accompaniments: wind that burst into the room followed by a fire ball that separated into flames that landed on each individual present. As the disciples were filled with the Holy Spirit, they began speaking in languages. (Acts 2:2-4) Quite a picture!

Tongues No. 1

This first manifestation of tongues is unique. There is no record in Scripture of a repeat of this particular miracle. Here's what happened: believers began praising God, but the words coming out of their mouths were a KNOWN FOREIGN LANGUAGE. Visitors from various other nations heard their own speech being spoken by these unlearned disciples (Acts 2:8). At least fifteen known languages were spoken that day beyond native Hebrew. It appears the disciples were praising God in Hebrew, but the words somehow were heard in various languages. Was the miracle in the speaking or the hearing? We do not know.

Tongues No. 2

The second manifestation of tongues is found in I Corinthians 12 and 14. This gift is an UTTERANCE IN THE CHURCH THAT REQUIRES INTERPRETATION (I Co. 12:10; 14:13; 14:27-28). In the "Acts 2" variety of tongues, no interpretation is needed because it is in a language that someone present recognized. This second kind of tongues amounts to a prophetic message that comes initially in the form of an unknown tongue but requires interpretation in order for the church to benefit (I Co. 14:5). The speaker does not understand what he or she is saying, and an interpretation is necessary to bring benefit.

Tongues No. 3
The third and last kind of tongues is purely private and is a PRAYER LANGUAGE. Paul describes this in I Corinthians 14 when he says, *"He who speaks in tongues does not speak to man but to God"* (I Co. 14:2). He goes on to say, *"...in the spirit he speaks mysteries to God."* He who speaks in tongues is edifying himself (14:4); his spirit prays (14:14; he blesses with the spirit (14:16); he *"gives thanks well"* (14:17). Scripture says his understanding is unfruitful, but he builds himself up on the inside (14:14).

Most instances of tongues in the Book of Acts after chapter 2 are this third kind. We have no record of known languages being spoken after Acts 2, nor are there examples of tongues being accompanied by an interpretation. We only read of individuals being filled with the Holy Spirit and speaking in tongues. I believe that the expression of tongues in Acts AFTER Pentecost are uniformly a PRAYER LANGUAGE and not a known language.

Pentecostal theology has concluded that the biblical formula for receiving the Spirit is the experience of speaking in tongues. While I acknowledge the availability of a prayer language, there is no mandate that tongues is exclusively the "initial evidence."

Will Everyone Speak in Tongues?
When Paul asked his rhetorical question in I Corinthians 12: *"Do all speak with tongues?"* (12:30), we do not know which manifestation of tongues he was referencing. We can however answer his question based on Scripture and experience.

1. Will everyone speak in tongues in the fashion of Acts 2?

Will they, under the influence of the Holy Spirit, speak a foreign, unknown language such as Hebrew, Spanish, or Russian? I can confidently declare "NO." It is not a reasonable expectation that every believer will at some time speak in tongues in this manner. I regularly pray in a prayer language, but have never spoken in a tongue identified as a foreign language, nor do I expect to ever do so.

2. Will every believer speak in tongues in the open congregation in such a way as to be interpreted by someone else?

Once again, "NO." Even though the Bible says that *"You can all prophesy"* (14:31), it is not reasonable to expect that everyone will at some time deliver a prophetic word to an individual or to the church. Even more so, tongues plus interpretation is not a defining marker of Christian Spirit-filled life.

3. Will every believer have and use a prayer language?

It is at this point that I must answer both "YES" and "NO." Will every believer use their prayer language? Unfortunately, the answer is "NO." But, I must add that I believe that every person who has the Holy Spirit alive inside of them has the ability to pray in an unknown tongue and COULD do so. All CAN pray in tongues, but not all WILL do so. The availability is there whereas there may never be occasion for the development of that gift.

What Happens When We Pray in Tongues?

Because we are three parts, we need to understand where tongues comes from and how it operates. I Thessalonians 5:23 says that we are spirit, soul, and body. Another way of describing this is that we are spiritual beings that have a mind and live in a body. We are primarily spiritual in nature. Our identity comes out of spiritual reality, not soulish, mental ideas. It is in your spirit that salvation arrives. This is the first step in the redemption of your entire being.

Similarly, the Bible says that your spirit can pray. Your spirit can communicate. This can at times come through your mental processes but at other times it supersedes or by-passes your mental being. Paul says it this way, *"I will pray with my spirit, and I will pray with my understanding."* (14:15)

This may sound crazy or irrational, but let's think further. Salvation is not purely a mental process. No doubt revelation comes from God in intelligible fashion, but our deepest spiritual encounters are not primarily intellectual exercises. They are spiritual in nature and transcend our understanding. Few, perhaps no, people understand fully what is happening to them when they are born again. It can take a lifetime to unpack the workings of saving grace.

When your spirit prays, the deepest essence is described by Paul as *"groanings which cannot be uttered"* (Rom. 8:26). There is a deep movement in the core of your being, in your spirit. It is not primarily emotional, although it may stir your emotions. It is not primarily intelligible, although it may stimulate profound insights. In fact, Paul says we *"do not know what to pray for as we ought"* (Rom. 8:26). The working of the Spirit goes beyond our mental processes.

Tongues have been attacked as being anti-intellectual, irrational, and therefore crazy. "Why would someone want to babble gibberish like a baby?" we are asked. "What is the benefit of irrational gobble-de-goop?" Consider, however, the nature and frequency of non-intelligible utterance.

Anytime you get good news, you are prone to make some sort of vocal response. It might be anything from a shout of glee to a sigh of relief. Go to any sporting event and watch what happens when the team wins a close one. Fans will shout and roar their approval. From deep inside themselves they release their joy, approval, gratitude, pleasure, and a whole host of other emotions.

Lovers may simply gaze into each other's eyes and, without uttering a word, express the deepest aspects of love and affection. There are ways of communicating that at times do not include formal intellectual mental processes.

I believe this, in essence, is what praying in tongues involves. Energized by the Holy Spirit, our own spirit begins to communicate with God from the deepest inner part of our being. In conjunction with the Holy Spirit, we release praise, love, petition, and worship to God. That is what praying in tongues is.

In this light, I have often found people to be surprised about tongues. They think of it as some sort of automatic, robotic takeover by God. They even refer to it as ecstatic – something like an "out-of-body experience." Tongues however is the very natural release of spiritual communication to God that may pass through the vocal apparatus as anything from groans to syllables to praise. In fact, those moments in corporate worship in which the deep bursts of love and affection for God can release tears of gratitude – those moments are very akin to a prayer language. It is beautiful.

SHOULD EVERYONE PRAY IN TONGUES?

So let's go further. Will everyone speak in tongues? The answer is NO. Can everyone speak in tongues? If you are referring to a prayer language, my answer is that every born-again believer CAN pray in tongues if they so desire.

So, should they pray in tongues? I agree at this point with the apostle Paul. *"I wish you all spoke with tongues,"* that is, use your prayer language (I Corinthians 14:5). Is this, however, a requirement? NO, absolutely not. Is it a marker of spiritual progress? NO. I know numerous spiritually immature believers who pray in tongues regularly. Tongues is not a marker of maturity. Is it important that I pray in tongues? YES. It is an incredible tool and weapon to be used for spiritual growth and advance. In fact, praying in the Spirit is listed among the spiritual armor of Ephesians 6 (Eph. 6:18).

Discussion Questions:

1. Do you believe God works supernaturally in our day, or is everything explainable by natural science?
2. Which of the gifts of the Holy Spirit as listed in I Corinthians 12:8-10 are most interesting to you?
3. Have you ever witnessed God do a verified miracle?
4. Why is spiritual language such a controversial gift?
5. What does it mean to "pray in the Spirit" or to "sing in the Spirit?" (see I Corinthians 14:15)

CHAPTER 5
Walking in the Spirit

EVIDENCES OF THE SPIRIT-EMPOWERED LIFE

THE EVIDENCES OF THE SPIRIT-FILLED, Spirit-empowered life are two-fold: Gifts and Fruit. Both are important. While the gifts are the fireworks, the fruit of the Spirit are the truest indicators of the Spirit's presence. We vitally need both. We must have both.

There must not be a battle between these two. Gifts represent power ministry. Fruit represents the water in which we swim. Fruit are our mode of operation. Without evidenced fruit, the gifts of the Spirit are empty (I Co. 13:1-3).

It is far too easy for Evangelical Christians to retreat to the fruit and claim excellent character that seemingly trumps supernatural power. This is a false dilemma! We do not need to choose between loving one another and seeing God's miraculous power.

The "prosperity gospel" has hindered us here. Far too many evangelical Christians think "Spirit-filled" believers only think you can be healed and enriched – and who cares about telling the truth? Therefore, they reject the entire Spirit-empowered life in favor of a life of endurance and suffering – and character.

Character and charisma are not in opposition! They are parallel lines along which the Kingdom of God runs.

It is no accident that I Corinthians 12 and 14 (which deal with the gifts of the Spirit) are bookends of I Corinthians 13 (which eloquently describes the fruit of the Spirit). Paul shouts to us:

...earnestly desire the best gifts. And yet I show you a more excellent way. I Corinthians 12:30

Zealously Desire...

Zealously desire to excel in the gifts (tongues, prophecy, healing, casting out demons, and all the rest of the fireworks). But make sure you walk in the Spirit. Make sure you move in the love of God. Make sure you do excellent ministry in an excellent way. We are to eagerly and fervently desire both fruit and gifts.

The cultivation of the fruit of the Spirit is central to walking with Jesus. We find them listed in Galatians 5:22-23.

[22] But the fruit of the Spirit is love, joy, peace, longsuffering, kindness, goodness, faithfulness, [23] gentleness, self-control. Against such there is no law. Galatians 5:22-23

This is a cavalcade of Christian character. In the pursuit of the supernatural, many have forgotten these virtues in favor of immediate experience. "If it feels good, it must be good." "Who cares so long as I get healed or delivered or anointed?"

The history of the Church is littered with faulty figures who carried the power of God. Much like Samson of old, they wield impressive GIFTS while exhibiting few FRUIT.

This is not a treatise on scolding the Church for failures of character. This is an endeavor to encourage the life of the Spirit. I will not belabor the need for integrity alongside fabulous gifting. But, I will conclude this section by giving this admonition.

God wants to empower His Church just as He did in the Book of Acts. He wants to fill every believer with the richness of the Holy Spirit promise. It is available today.

DISCUSSION QUESTIONS:

1. Why are the fruit of the Spirit important to us as we grow in empowerment from God?
2. Do you have friends who can help you grow in character in Christ?
3. What steps can you take to grow in the fruit of the Spirit?

Conclusion: the Comforter has Come

Through 2000 years of church history, there have been seasons of great success, and there have been decades of decline. There have been times when the church was a shining city on a hill. Then, there were times when the candle of God's light nearly flickered out.

Our own individual lives can be like this, too. In the grand days of growth and advance we feel like no one can stop us. But in the deep valleys of hard times, a feather could knock us over.

What can keep the church strong? What can keep each of us strong? Jesus Christ points us to His own prescription for powerful, steady, prevailing life! He gave the Holy Spirit a name which we often translate Comforter or Helper[8]. It is the Greek word *paraclete*. The literal meaning of this wonderful word is "one called alongside to help."[9] In His unique role, the Holy Spirit comes alongside us to strengthen us, steady us, encourage us, and cheer us on to success.

We might ask, "How strong is Jesus?" Obviously, He was strong enough to endure all sorts of up's and down's. He was courageous enough to overcome the Cross. He was faith-filled enough to walk

---

8 John 14:16-18, 25-31; 15:26; and 16:5-15;
9 Bauer, Walter, William F. Arndt and F. Wilbur Gingrich, *A Greek-English Lexicon of the New Testament* (Chicago: University of Chicago Press, 1957), pgs. 622-623.

on water. He was able to sleep peacefully through storms. He embodied life in this fallen world as God says it can be lived.

The role of the Holy Spirit is to take the riches of Christ and APPLY them to us. Jesus Himself described it this way:

> *He (the Holy Spirit) will honor and glorify Me, because He will take of (receive, draw upon) what is Mine and will reveal (declare, disclose, transmit) it to you.* John 16:14 (Amplified)

Did you get that? The job of the Holy Spirit is to take what belongs to Jesus and transfer it – transmit it – to us! We can, by the power of the Holy Spirit, be as steady as Jesus.

Ours can be a God-saturated, joy-filled life. That's why Paul tells us to no longer settle for the cheap substitutes but go for the real thing. He invites you today:

> *[18] And do not be drunk with wine, in which is dissipation; but* **be filled with the Spirit,** *[19] speaking to one another in psalms and hymns and spiritual songs, singing and making melody in your heart to the Lord,* Ephesians 5:18-19 (NKJV)

Of particular note, the original Greek tense for "be filled" in this verse, is present continuous. Dr. Francis Foulkes, in his commentary on Ephesians, says, "The practical implication is that the Christian is to leave his life open to be filled *constantly and repeatedly* by the divine Spirit."[10] (my emphasis)

May the Lord fill each of us with more of Himself. May the Holy Spirit become our constant companion. May Jesus become more real to us as the Holy Spirit rests on our way. May the Spirit-filled life be a reality that brings power, blessing, and joy unspeakable. The Comforter has come.

---

10 Foulkes, Francis. *The Epistle of Paul to the Ephesians* (Grand Rapids, Michigan: William B. Eerdmans, 1976), p. 152

Conclusion: the Comforter has Come

Discussion Questions:

1. Why do you think we need to regularly be "re-filled" and re-charged with the Holy Spirit?
2. How is the Holy Spirit a comfort and help to you?

BIBLIOGRAPHY

Bauer, Walter, William F. Arndt and F. Wilbur Gingrich. *A Greek-English Lexicon of the New Testament.* Chicago: University of Chicago Press, 1957.

Bennett, Dennis and Rita. *Trinity of Man.* Plainfield, NJ: Logos International, 1979.

Dunn, James D.G. *Baptism in the Holy Spirit.* Philadelphia: Westminster Press, 1970.

Foulkes, Francis. *The Epistle of Paul to the Ephesians.* Grand Rapids, Michigan: William B. Eerdmans Publishing, 1976

Nee, Watchman. *The Spiritual Man.* New York: Christian Fellowship Publishers, 1968.

Stott, John R.W. *Baptism & Fullness: the Work of the Holy Spirit Today.* Downers Grove, IL: Intervarsity Press, 1964.

Vine, W.E. *Vine's Expository Dictionary of New Testament Words.* McLean, VA: McDonald Publishing Co.

Made in United States
North Haven, CT
22 January 2025